W0224212

Peter Foreman

Jack the Ripper

Editors: Frances Evans, Emma Berridge
Design and art direction: Nadia Maestri
Computer graphics: Simona Corniola
Illustrations: Didi Coppola
Picture research: Laura Lagomarsino

First edition: January 2005

Picture credits:
© Bettmann/CONTRASTO: 5; *bfi* Stills: 6, 7; © Hulton-Deutsch Collection/CONTRASTO: 32, 60; Christopher Wood Gallery, London, UK/Bridgeman Art Library: 33; Sheffield Galleries and Museums Trust, UK/Bridgeman Art Library: 58; Mary Evans Picture Library: 59; Visit London Corporate: 61.

We would be happy to receive your comments and suggestions, and give you any other information concerning our material.
info@blackcat-cideb.com
blackcat-cideb.com

CISQ CISQCERT
TEXTBOOKS AND TEACHING MATERIALS
The quality of the publisher's design, production and sales processes has been certified to the standard of
UNI EN ISO 9001

ISBN 978-88-530-0320-1 Book + CD

Printed in Italy by Litoprint, Genoa

CONTENTS

FCE First Certificate in English Examination-style exercises

T: GRADE 7 Trinity-style exercises (Grade 7)

This story is recorded in full.

These symbols indicate the beginning and end of the extracts linked to the listening activities.

The 1880s: *A Creative Decade*

1887 was the year of Queen Victoria's Golden Jubilee, when the British celebrated fifty years of the monarch's reign and the success of the British Empire. But there were many other reasons for celebration because the 1880s was a decade of new inventions and products that are still with us today.

For example, the bicycle. John Starley manufactured the first modern bicycle, the Rover, in 1885. Three years later John Boyd Dunlop developed the pneumatic tyre, which had a tube of air inside it. And it was in 1885 that the German Karl Benz constructed a three-wheeled vehicle, *Motorwagen*, that used petrol – and the age of the car began.

A product that is now famous all over the world first appeared in 1886. It was called Coca-Cola. 1888 was the year when Emile Berliner invented a gramophone that played discs – the first records! In the same year George Eastman sold his Kodak box cameras, the first camera that you could hold in your hand. And think of all the synthetic materials we wear today. The first artificial fibre, a kind of silk, was introduced and produced in England by Joseph Swan in 1883.

1886 saw the publication of R. L. Stevenson's *Dr Jekyll and Mr Hyde.* A stage play based on the book became very popular in 1888. It continued for weeks until September, when the manager suddenly decided to stop it because some horrible murders of women in Whitechapel were causing panic.

His Master's Voice advertisement.

The year before this, 1887, Sir Arthur Conan Doyle introduced to the world a super-detective. His name was Sherlock Holmes. Of course he was only a character in fiction, but perhaps this legendary detective was the only man who could solve the greatest mystery in the history of crime – the identity of the so-called Jack the Ripper, the murderer of women in Whitechapel.

1 **Write briefly what happened in the following years, like the example.**

1883 First artificial fibre produced

1885 ....

1886 ....

1887 ....

1888 ....

2 **What do you know about the story of Jack the Ripper? Have you seen any of the films on the following pages?**

Filmography

There are many films about Jack the Ripper.[1] Most of them are not very accurate, others are sensationalist and absurd. The following is a selection.

Man in the Attic. 1953. Directed by Hugo Fregonese, starring Jack Palance. Jack the Ripper is a mysterious lodger. Not a new idea, but Jack Palance makes a very good Ripper.

A Study in Terror. 1965. Directed by James Hill, starring John Neville, Donald Houston. The great Sherlock Holmes discovers the identity of Jack the Ripper.

A scene from **A Study in Terror** (1965).

1. **Ripper** : (here) murderer who moves forcefully and rapidly.

Time after Time. 1980. Directed by Nicholas Meyer, starring Malcolm McDowell, David Warner. The Ripper escapes from London in 1888 in a time machine built by H. G. Wells, the famous author, who follows Jack and catches him.

Jack the Ripper. 1988. Directed by David Wickes, starring Michael Caine, Armand Assante. Inspector Abbeline discovers that the Ripper is the American actor Richard Mansfield, who is performing in *Dr Jekyll and Mr Hyde.*

The Ripper. 1997. Directed by Janet Meyers, starring Patrick Bergin, Michael York. The conclusion that the Ripper is Prince Albert Victor, son of Queen Victoria, is said by many to be completely wrong.

From Hell. 2001. Directed by Allen Hughes and Albert Hughes, starring Johnny Depp as an absurdly young and handsome Inspector Abbeline, who is an opium addict. He has a love affair with Mary Kelly, one of the Ripper's victims.

A scene from **From Hell** (2001).

CHAMPION

1 Scene

Look at the scene of London in the 1880s on pages 8 and 9. What are these people doing?

a. The boy with the newspapers.

b. The man with the basket.

c. The man and the woman on the right.

d. The three boys in the background.

2 What can you say about the differences in their clothes and appearance?

Before you read

2 FCE

1 Listening

Listen to the beginning of Chapter One and complete the sentences.

1 At 9 o'clock that night a great fire .... the sky to a deep red.

2 From Whitechapel hundreds of people ....

3 The poorest people lived .... in doorways.

4 People drank alcohol because .... and helped them to feel better.

5 Mary Ann needed the money to pay for a bed, but she also needed alcohol, and she ....

6 She had to leave Cooley's because ....

7 The streets of Whitechapel were dark and gloomy because they ....

8 When Mary Ann's friend Ellen saw her .... , Mary Ann was drunk.

9 After Mary Ann left her friend Ellen, only one ....

CHAPTER **ONE**

MURDER IN BUCK'S ROW[1]

London in the year 1888. On August 30th the weather was cool, the sky was black with smoke from domestic fires, and rain fell; rain and more rain. The late summer and autumn had the heaviest rain of the year.

At 9 o'clock on that Thursday night a great fire in London Docks changed the colour of the sky in the East End of London to a deep red. From the dirty streets, dark passages and slum houses [2] of Whitechapel hundreds of people went to watch the fire. Many of them were poor and homeless. They lived and slept in squalid lodging houses. [3] The poorest lived in the streets and slept in doorways. [4]

As always, the pubs were crowded and noisy. Alcohol was cheap and it helped people to feel better. Mary Ann Nichols was in 'The

1. **Row** : number of houses in a line, like a street.
2. **slum houses** : houses in a very bad condition, in a very poor part of a city.
3. **lodging houses** : (here) accommodation for poor, homeless people, who paid for a bed or room.
4. **doorways** : entrances to buildings or rooms.

Frying Pan' pub on the corner of Brick Lane, spending her last pennies on drink. She needed the money to pay for a bed in the 'White House', her lodging house in Flower and Dean Street. But Mary Ann needed alcohol too, and she was drinking too much. Later that night she tried to get a bed at Cooley's lodging house in Thrawl Street, but she had to leave because she had no money. So she walked around the wet, cold streets hoping to earn something. One of the poorest areas in London, Whitechapel did not have many street lamps. The streets were dark, gloomy and dangerous.

Mary Ann Nichols was still walking the streets when her friend Ellen Holland saw her at 2.30 a.m. on August 31st. By that time Mary Ann — known as Polly — was very drunk. The women talked for a few minutes. Ellen asked Polly to come with her to the lodgings in Thrawl Street. But Polly went away along Whitechapel Road to try and get some money. After that only one person saw her alive again — her killer. END

Buck's Row was a quiet, narrow road with warehouses [1] on one side and some small houses or cottages on the other. At the end of the cottages was the entrance to Brown's stableyard, [2] and then the long wall of a school. The street had only one gas lamp. At nearly 3.40 in the morning it was dark.

At this hour Charles Cross, a carman, [3] was walking to work. He came into Buck's Row from Brady Street. A few moments later he noticed something on the pavement in front of Brown's stableyard, and crossed the road. He saw that it was a woman. At that moment he heard footsteps. It was another carman, Robert

1. **warehouses** : buildings where items for sale in shops or markets are stored.
2. **stableyard** : open area surrounded by stables where horses are kept.
3. **carman** : man who drove a cart and horse, usually for markets.

Paul, also on his way to work. Cross asked him to come and look. The men looked at the woman, but in the darkness they did not know if she was drunk or dead. They decided to continue on their way to work and tell the first policeman they met.

They saw a policeman, Constable [1] Jonas Mizen, not far away in Baker's Row, told him about the woman, and then walked on to work. When Constable Mizen arrived at the gates of the stableyard, another policeman, Constable John Neil, was already there. He had a lantern, and he showed Constable Mizen a deep cut in the woman's neck.

'I passed this place at 3.15,' Constable Neil said, 'but there was nothing here.'

'The woman's legs are still warm,' said Constable Mizen. 'I think Mr Cross interrupted her killer.'

Opposite the stableyard stood a warehouse. The manager, Walter Purkiss, and his wife were in their bedroom on the second floor. Mrs Purkiss was awake most of the night, and Mr Purkiss slept badly and was awake between one and two o'clock, but they heard nothing. Mrs Emma Green lived in the cottage next to the stableyard; she did not hear anything either. Polly Nichols's killer worked quickly and silently, and disappeared like a ghost. He probably ran into Whitechapel Road through a narrow lane called Wood's Buildings.

Polly Nichols died just a few days after her forty-third birthday. She was about 1.58m tall, and had dark brown hair. She was wearing a blue dress, black woollen stockings, [2] men's boots, and a black straw bonnet. [3] She had a comb, a white handkerchief, and a

1. **Constable** : police officer of the lowest rank.
2. **stockings** : long socks for women.
3. **bonnet** : woman's hat fixed with ribbons under the chin.

broken piece of looking-glass. These were all the possessions she had. Polly was an 'Unfortunate': a polite Victorian word for a prostitute. She was probably an alcoholic. She lived in workhouses [1] and, when she had the money to pay, in lodging houses. In December 1887 she was sleeping in Trafalgar Square. Her friend Ellen said she was a clean, quiet person. And her father said, 'I don't think she had any enemies. She was too good for that.'

When Dr Llewellyn examined the body, he thought the killer was right-handed. The man probably strangled [2] Polly first, put her on the ground, and cut her throat. The police had no other clues to help them find the killer. There was also no obvious motive, such as robbery. This was a new, unknown type of murder, which they could not understand. Polly Nichols was not the first 'Unfortunate' who was murdered that year, so Scotland Yard [3] chiefs sent their most experienced officer to investigate. This was Inspector Abbeline, a fine detective who knew the East End and its people very well. But he did not know that this killer was different – clever, efficient, and savage. Today he is probably the most famous killer in the world, Jack the Ripper. But nobody has ever discovered his true identity.

On August 31st the *Star* newspaper had a sensational headline:

A REVOLTING [4] MURDER

ANOTHER WOMAN FOUND HORRIBLY MUTILATED IN WHITECHAPEL

GHASTLY [5] CRIMES BY A MANIAC

1. **workhouses** : public institutions where poor people worked for food and accommodation.
2. **strangled** : killed by pressing hands around the throat.
3. **Scotland Yard** : official central police offices.
4. **revolting** : horrible and disgusting.
5. **ghastly** : extremely unpleasant.

Go back to the text

1 Answer these questions.

a. Why were there domestic fires on August 30th?
b. What happened in London Docks at 9 o'clock?
c. Where did homeless people sleep if they had the money?
d. How did Mary Ann Nichols spend her last pennies?
e. Why didn't Whitechapel have many street lamps?
f. What time did Ellen Holland last see Mary Ann (Polly) alive?
g. Where in Buck's Row did Charles Cross discover the body?
h. Who did the carmen meet in Baker's Row?
i. Where were Mr and Mrs Purkiss at the time of the murder?
j. Who said Polly was clean and quiet?
k. How did the Ripper kill Polly Nichols?
l. Why couldn't the police understand the murder?

2 Setting

A Use the information in Chapter One to number the boxes on the map.

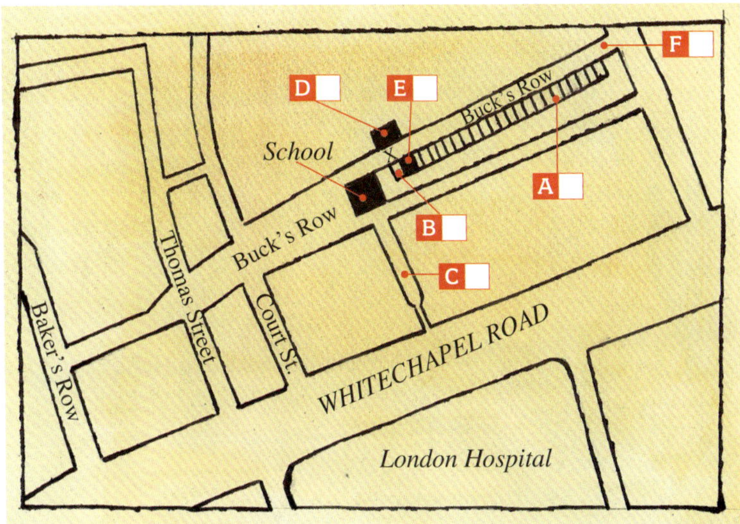

1. Brown's stableyard
2. Emma Green's house
3. Warehouse
4. Cottages
5. Charles Cross's route to work
6. Wood's Buildings

B What happened at the following places?

1. ....
3. ....
6. ....

FCE **3** **Read the text and choose the correct word for each space. Write A, B, C or D in each space, like the example.**

(**0**) ..B.......... 1888 Whitechapel was a very (**1**) .... area with (**2**) .... slums and homeless people. They lived in the streets, or in lodging houses (**3**) .... they were lucky. In the (**4**) .... streets lived vagabonds, thieves, and (**5**) .... kind of criminal. (**6**) .... weren't many gas lamps in the streets, (**7**) .... thieves could attack and (**8**) .... people in (**9**) .... dark, and (**10**) .... escape easily. Whitechapel was a perfect place for Jack the Ripper!

0	**A** At	**B** In	**C** On	**D** To
1	**A** rich	**B** beautiful	**C** poor	**D** clean
2	**A** a lot of	**B** little	**C** any	**D** much
3	**A** so	**B** because	**C** as	**D** if
4	**A** main	**B** back	**C** high	**D** wide
5	**A** all	**B** many	**C** one	**D** every
6	**A** They	**B** There	**C** It	**D** We
7	**A** because	**B** but	**C** so	**D** then
8	**A** steal	**B** rob	**C** destroy	**D** help
9	**A** a lot of	**B** a	**C** the	**D** some
10	**A** then	**B** after	**C** next	**D** as

4 Vocabulary

A **Can you find some words from the text to describe the following?**

a. Polly Nichols's killer ....
b. Polly Nichols ....
c. The weather on August 30th 1888 ....
d. The streets of Whitechapel ....
e. The pubs ....
f. Buck's Row ....

B What do the following adjectives describe?

a. dirty ....
b. poor, homeless ....
c. squalid ....
d. cheap ....
e. black, red ....
f. experienced ....

5 Characters

Look at these pictures of some of the people in Chapter One. Write their names below the pictures. Then write what they did.

1. .... 2. .... 3. ....

a. .... b. .... c. ....

4. .... 5. .... 6. ....

d. .... e. .... f. ....

6 Summary

In his statement Charles Cross described how he found the body. Put the sentences in the correct order. Write 1, 2, 3, etc. in the boxes.

a. ☐ I crossed the road.
b. ☐ At about 3.40 I came into Buck's Row from Brady Street.
c. ☐ At that moment Robert Paul came along.
d. ☐ On the morning of August 31st I was on my way to work.
e. ☐ I asked him to come and look.
f. ☐ Then I saw something on the pavement in front of Brown's stableyard.
g. ☐ It was dark so we couldn't tell if the woman was drunk or dead.
h. ☐ I saw a woman on the ground.
i. ☐ We decided to go and find a policeman.
j. ☐ We saw Constable Mizen in Baker's Row and told him about the woman.

7 Writing a report

Constable Neil found the body a few minutes later. Can you briefly write his report?

Begin like this:

On the morning of Friday August 31st I was on my usual beat.[1] At 3.15 a.m. ...

1. **beat** : regular route walked by a policeman.

Before you read

FCE **1** **Listening**

3

Listen to the beginning of Chapter Two. For questions 1-5, choose the best answer, A, B, or C. Put a tick (✓) in the correct box.

1 Hanbury Street
- **A** ☐ goes from Commercial Street to Baker's Row.
- **B** ☐ is short.
- **C** ☐ is a long way from Buck's Row.

2 Mrs Richardson
- **A** ☐ made some money by renting rooms to people.
- **B** ☐ lived in three rooms on the ground floor.
- **C** ☐ had a shop in the cellar.

3 John Davis's room
- **A** ☐ had three people in it.
- **B** ☐ was at the top of the house.
- **C** ☐ had a view of the backyard.

4 Number 29
- **A** ☐ had 70 people in it.
- **B** ☐ was next to a shop.
- **C** ☐ was old and crowded.

5 How did people enter number 29 from Hanbury Street?
- **A** ☐ through Mrs Hardiman's shop
- **B** ☐ through a door at the back
- **C** ☐ through a door next to a shop

CHAPTER **TWO**

MURDER IN THE LIGHT OF DAY

3 Hanbury Street is a long street that goes from Commercial Street to Baker's Row, not far from Buck's Row. Now demolished, number 29 was an old building with three floors. On the ground floor [1] Mrs Hardiman had a cat meat shop. On the first floor Mrs Richardson and her grandson lived in three rooms, and she let out [2] the other rooms. She also had a packing case business [3] in the cellar at the back of the house. Her son, John, helped her in the business but he did not live in Hanbury Street. A carman, John Davis, occupied the attic at the front with his wife and three sons. A total of seventeen poor people lived in number 29, which was a crowded, busy place. From Hanbury Street people entered the house through a door next to Mrs

1. **ground floor** : floor of a building at street level.
2. **let out** : rented to people for money.
3. **packing case business** : commercial activity for making large containers to transport goods or other materials.

Hardiman's shop. The door opened to a passage about 7-8 metres long. At the end of the passage there was a door to the backyard. [1] This was where Jack the Ripper murdered another woman in the early hours of September 8th.

It was about 4.45 a.m. when John Richardson arrived at number 29. On his way to work at Spitalfields market he often checked the passage because strangers sometimes came in. This morning he also wanted to check the cellar [2] door at the back. Some time before thieves broke the lock and stole things. John walked through the passage and opened the door to the yard. Then he sat on some stone steps and took off one of his boots, which was hurting his toe. He cut a piece of leather from the boot with a knife. It was getting light and he could see that the lock on the cellar door was secure. There was nobody in the yard. John left the house and went to the market.

Albert Cadosch, a carpenter, lived at 27 Hanbury Street, next to number 29. He got up at 5.15 a.m. and in a few minutes he went out to the backyard. He was returning to the house when he heard a voice in the next yard say 'No'. Three or four minutes later Albert came into the yard again and heard a sound like a bump [3] against the wooden fence [4] that separated the yards of numbers 27 and 29. He thought it was somebody falling against the fence, but he did not look to see what it was. Then he left for work and passed Spitalfields Church at about 5.32 a.m.

1. **backyard** : area of enclosed ground behind a house.
2. **cellar** : space or room below ground level in a house.
3. **bump** : quiet sound made by a collision or impact.
4. **fence** : barrier between two gardens or yards.

JACK THE RIPPER

At 5.45 a.m. John Davis got up. By six o'clock he was ready for work and went downstairs to the backyard. From the top of the steps he saw a horrible sight. On his left between the steps and the wooden fence lay the mutilated body of a woman. Davis ran out into Hanbury Street, where he saw some workmen and shouted, 'Men, come here!' They followed him, looked at the body from the steps, then ran to find a policeman.

Inspector Joseph Chandler was on duty in Commercial Street at 6.10 a.m. when some workmen rushed [1] towards him and told him about the dead woman. Chandler arrived at number 29 and noted down that the woman was lying on her back, with a deep cut from left to right across her throat and mutilations to her stomach. The inspector saw a piece of muslin [2] and two small combs that the murderer had put near her feet. The killer also took some rings from her finger. The victim was 1.52m tall. She had dark brown hair and blue eyes. Two lower front teeth were missing. Her clothes were all old and dirty: a long black jacket down to her knees, petticoats, [3] stockings, a black skirt, and boots. Who was she?

Annie Chapman – or Dark Annie to her friends – was 47 years old. Her history told a sad story. Once she had children, but one died and another was disabled. Annie drank a lot and her marriage broke down. The small sum of money which she received from her husband stopped when he died in 1886. Annie worked when possible, selling flowers or making clothes. Sometimes she borrowed money from her relatives. But her

1. **rushed** : ran quickly.
2. **muslin** : thin cotton material.
3. **petticoats** : skirts worn under a woman's dress.

taste for alcohol dominated her life, and eventually she had to walk the streets as a prostitute.

Let us follow Annie's movements before the night of her murder. She lived in a lodging house and paid eight pennies a night. But the week before her murder she was not at the lodging house. She had a fight with a woman about a piece of soap and got a black eye. When she met her friend Amelia Palmer on September 2nd and 3rd she showed her the black eye and a bruise[1] on her face. The next day she told Amelia she did not feel well. She looked pale, so Amelia gave her two pennies to buy something to eat. 'Don't spend it on rum,' she told Annie. Amelia saw Annie for the last time on the 7th. 'I must get some money or I can't sleep in my lodgings,' Annie said.

At about 1.30 a.m. on September 8th Annie was in the kitchen of her lodging house, eating potatoes and talking with the other lodgers. She told the deputy that she did not have any money, but asked him to keep her bed because she wanted to return with the money. She left at about 1.50. Nobody saw her alive again; she never came back for her bed.

Two people were important witnesses in the murder case. One, Albert Cadosch, heard a voice in the yard and a sound like that of somebody falling against the fence between 5.20 to 5.30 a.m. The other, Elizabeth Darrell, said that as she was walking down Hanbury Street at about 5.30 a.m. on her way to Spitalfields market, she noticed a man and a woman talking outside number 29. She only saw the man's back, but she identified the woman as Annie Chapman later in the mortuary.

1. **bruise** : mark on skin caused by injury, i.e., a blow or impact.

29

JACK THE RIPPER

Mrs Darrell heard the man say, 'Will you?' and the woman reply, 'Yes'. Mrs Darrell could not describe the man very well. He had a dark complexion and was only a little taller than Annie. He wore a brown deerstalker hat [1] and a dark coat. She had the impression he was over forty and perhaps foreign.

We know that witnesses often make small errors in time, so the man Mrs Darrell saw was very probably the murderer, and he attacked Annie at approximately 5.30 a.m. On that morning the sun rose at 5.23. Spitalfields market opened at 5.00. It was a busy morning, with a lot of people already in the streets or getting up, and heavy traffic for the market. Five people in number 29 could see the murder scene from their windows. This time Jack the Ripper was in a dangerous situation. But again nobody saw or heard him when he killed Annie in the light of a busy day. And he escaped through the streets like a phantom. [2]

1. **deerstalker hat** : cloth hat with peaks at the front and back – as worn by Sherlock Holmes.
2. **phantom** : ghost; unreal or imagined thing.

Go back to the text

1 Summary

Match the two parts of the sentences to make a summary of Chapter Two. The first has been done for you.

1. ~~At 4.45 a.m. John Richardson arrived at 29 Hanbury Street~~
2. He sat on the steps in the backyard
3. Between about 5.20-5.30 Albert Cadosch
4. John Davis discovered the body
5. Then he and some workmen
6. Inspector Chandler saw a deep cut in the woman's throat
7. The victim was short
8. Annie had some bad luck in her life
9. For a week before her death Annie did not go to her lodging house
10. On September 8th she left the lodging house at 1.50 a.m.
11. At about 5.30 a.m. Mrs Darrell saw a man and a woman
12. The murderer probably killed Annie around 5.30

a. ☐ at about 6.00 a.m.
b. ☐ and cut some leather from his boot.
c. ☐ to get some money to pay for her bed.
d. ☐ and some objects on the ground near her feet.
e. ☐ talking outside number 29.
f. 1 to check the passage and cellar door.
g. ☐ when it was light and the streets were busy.
h. ☐ with dark brown hair and blue eyes.
i. ☐ heard a voice say 'No' and a bump against the fence.
j. ☐ because she had a black eye and bruises from a fight.
k. ☐ ran to find a policeman.
l. ☐ and began to drink too much.

Relative clauses

Defining relative clause:

Hanbury Street is a long street ***that runs between Commercial Street and Baker's Row.***

Defining relative clauses also define people.

Subject: *John Davis was the person* ***who discovered the body.***
Object: *The man (who)* ***Mrs Darrell saw*** *had a dark complexion.*

In the second example 'who' is not necessary because it is the object of the verb in the relative clause. Note that sentences with defining relative clauses do not have a comma.

Non-defining relative clauses do not define the noun; they give more information about it so they are not essential.

Subject: *Number 29 was in Hanbury Street. It was a crowded place.*
Number 29, ***which was a crowded place****, was in Hanbury Street.*

Object: *Seventeen people lived at number 29. It was a crowded place.*
Seventeen people lived at number 29, ***which was a crowded place.***

Note that in non-defining relative clauses commas are necessary.

These clauses can also add information about people.

Subject: *Annie drank at lot. She was 47 years old.*
Annie, ***who drank a lot****, was 47 years old.*

Object: *The murderer killed Annie in daylight. Nobody saw or heard him.*
The murderer, ***who nobody saw or heard****, killed Annie in daylight.*

2 Join the sentences with a defining or non-defining relative clause to make one sentence.

a. The inspector saw some objects. The killer had put them near Annie's feet.
b. Mrs Richardson let out other rooms. She lived with her grandson.
c. The passage went through the house. It was 7-8 metres long.
d. John Richardson took off one of his boots. It was hurting his toe.
e. Annie Chapman was talking to a man. Mrs Darrell identified her later.

f. Jack the Ripper escaped through the streets. He was in a dangerous situation.

g. The attic room looked over Hanbury Street. John Davis occupied it.

h. The man was taller than Annie. Mrs Darrell saw him.

i. Annie met her friend Amelia Palmer. Amelia gave her two pennies.

j. Amelia Palmer gave her some money. Amelia was Annie's friend.

4 **3 Listening**

FCE **Listen to Mrs Darrell's statement and complete the sentences.**

METROPOLITAN POLICE STATEMENT

Name: Elizabeth Darrell

September 8th 1888

On Saturday September 8th I went to Spitalfields market. When I (1) .... Hanbury Street at 5.30 a.m., I (2) ....
They were talking (3) .... number 29. The woman was Annie Chapman but I (4) .... face. He said, '(5) .... ?' and the woman replied, 'Yes.' He was (6) ...., only a little taller (7) ....
He had a brown deerstalker hat and a (8) .... I think (9) .... forty, and his complexion was dark. I got the impression that he (10) ...., but I can't say why.
This statement is true.

Signed

Elizabeth Darrell

Life in the *East End*

The East End of London was already a poor area at the end of the 17th century when hundreds of refugees [1] arrived from France. They were silk weavers, and Spitalfields became a centre for the production of silk. During the 18th century rich silk merchants built beautiful houses. But the East End remained the home of the poor. In 1807 there were 15,000 people in Spitalfields, most of them poor. By the 1880s the conditions were so bad that Hanbury Street was in one of the better areas. The old weavers' houses were damp, [2] dirty, and ready for demolition. But they were still inhabited as squalid lodging

Backstreets of London from **London, a Pilgrimage** (1872) by Gustave Doré.

1. **refugees** : people forced to leave their country in order to escape war, persecution or natural disaster.
2. **damp** : slightly wet.

A London market (19th century) by Godefroy Durand.

houses or 'doss-houses'. 8,500 homeless people lived in 233 doss-houses. Sometimes sixty people lived and slept in nine rooms.

Many people worked in the markets. The largest and best Victorian street market was in Whitechapel. Everybody was buying or selling and the poor lived on the poor. Women made clothes all day in workshops where conditions were very bad. In 1888 there was a strike by the female workers about conditions in Bryant and May's match factory. Men worked in similar conditions in tanneries (making leather) or slaughterhouses (killing animals for meat). Carmen or carters like Charles Cross transported market produce in a horse and cart. There was an estimated population of 80,000 prostitutes.

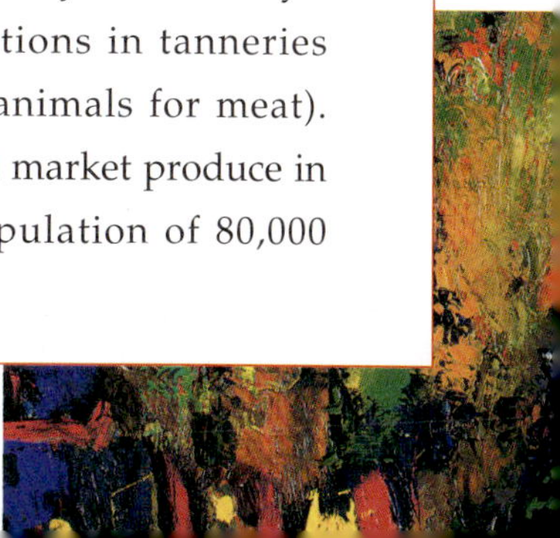

Life was hard in the East End. Two kilos of stale bread cost half a penny and lasted one family for a week. Water was often dirty – it was safer to drink beer or gin. In one street there was a single water pipe for sixteen houses. Many streets were badly-lit and full of dangerous criminals. The worst place was Dorset Street in Spitalfields. This was a crowded slum of beggars,[1] robbers, thieves, murderers, and ragged[2] children. The police never followed a criminal into Dorset Street alone. The East End was a perfect scenario for mystery and murder.

1 Which of the following statements are true (T) or false (F)? Correct the false ones.

	T	F
a. In the 18th century there was a silk industry in Spitalfields.	☐	☐
b. By the early 19th century the East End was a rich area.	☐	☐
c. During the 19th century the condition of the poor got better.	☐	☐
d. The lodging houses were old, damp and overcrowded.	☐	☐
e. The working conditions in the East End were bad.	☐	☐
f. Most houses had a supply of clean water.	☐	☐
g. A family could eat well on half a penny a week.	☐	☐
h. Dorset Street was the most dangerous place in the East End.	☐	☐
i. Policemen never went into Dorset Street.	☐	☐
j. For a criminal like Jack the Ripper the East End was ideal.	☐	☐

1. **beggars** : people who live by asking for food and money.
2. **ragged** : wearing old and torn clothes.

Before you read

5 1 Listening – setting

Listen to the description of Dutfield's Yard at the beginning of Chapter Three and write 1, 2, 3, etc. in the correct box on the map. One is done for you.

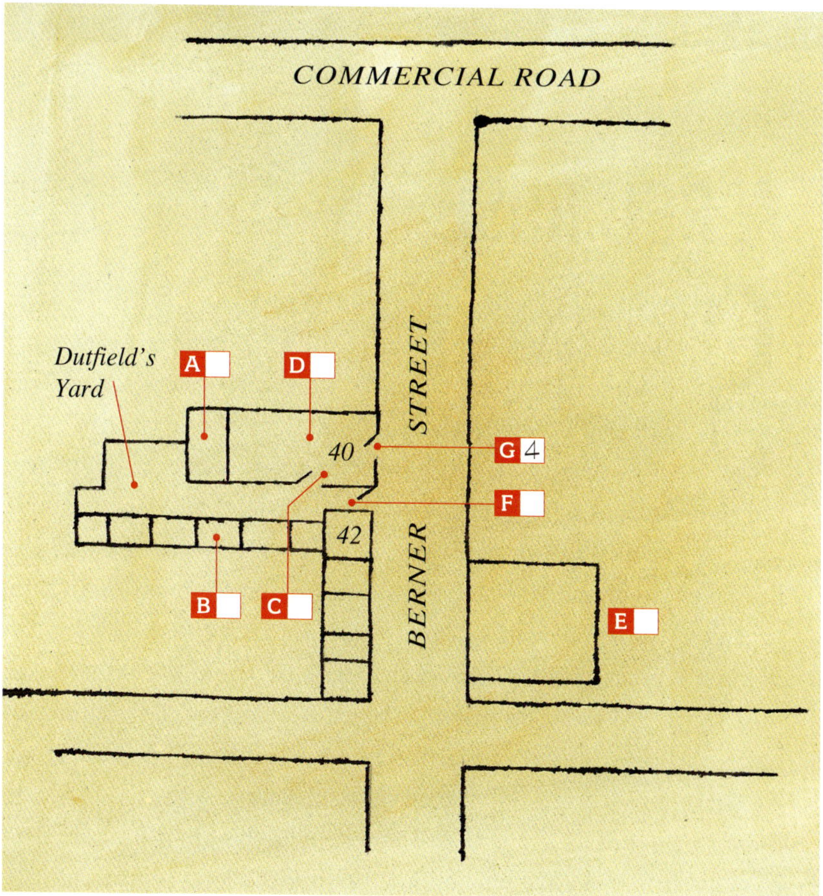

1. Entrance gates to Dutfield's Yard
2. School
3. International Workingmen's Educational Club
4. Front door of club
5. Kitchen door of club
6. Club office
7. Cottages

CHAPTER **THREE**

A RED ROSE

Sunday September 30th, 12.30 a.m. Berner Street, off Commercial Road, was quiet. Although the weather was wet and breezy,[1] it was a mild night.

In Berner Street, almost opposite a school, were two big wooden gates which opened into Dutfield's Yard, a dark, narrow court between numbers 42 and 40. Number 40 was the premises of[2] the International Workingmen's Educational Club. Just over half an hour before, Russian and Polish Jews were having a discussion in the club. Most of them went home at midnight. Twenty or more stayed behind in the clubroom upstairs. Some of them began singing Russian songs and dancing.

There was a front door to the club in Berner Street, and a side door in Dutfield's Yard that opened into the club kitchen. The passage into the yard was about five metres long and extremely dark. But inside the yard light came from the club windows, the club office, and from some cottages on the other side of the yard.

1. **breezy** : a little windy.
2. **premises of** : (here) building officially occupied by.

A RED ROSE

Constable William Smith's beat [1] took him along Berner Street every 25-30 minutes. At 12.35 a.m. he noticed a man and a woman by the school wall opposite Dutfield's Yard. The woman wore a red flower on her jacket. The man had a parcel wrapped in newspaper. [2] He was 1.70m tall, about 28 years old, and wore a deerstalker hat and dark clothes.

At 12.45 Israel Schwartz was walking towards Dutfield's Yard when he saw a man stop and speak to a woman in the entrance. Schwartz later described the man as 1.65m tall, about 30, with a small brown moustache. [3] He was wearing a dark jacket and trousers, and a black cap with a peak. [4] Suddenly the man pulled the woman into the street and threw her down on to the pavement. She screamed but not loudly. Schwartz did not want any trouble so he crossed to the other side of the street. There he saw another man, who was lighting a pipe. Then the first man shouted 'Lipski', perhaps at Schwartz, perhaps at the other man. Frightened, Schwartz ran away. The man with the pipe ran after him. Schwartz thought the man was following him, but a few moments later when he looked back, there was nobody behind him.

What was going on? Later, Inspector Abbeline had a good theory. He knew that Lipski was the name of a Jewish murderer, and in 1888 it was an insulting word used against Jews. Israel Schwartz was Jewish, so perhaps when the first man saw him, he shouted 'Lipski' to warn him aggressively to go away. Or perhaps he was warning the man with the pipe that Schwartz was

1. **beat** : regular route walked by a policeman.
2. **wrapped in newspaper** : covered with newspaper, like a package.
3. **moustache** : hair growing between the nose and mouth.
4. **peak** : piece that projects from the front of a cap.

coming. Was this man the murderer's accomplice? [1] Or was he an innocent witness who ran away like Schwartz?

At 1 a.m. Louis Diemschutz was coming along Berner Street with his pony and cart. He lived with his wife at the club, which they managed together. When he drove his cart into the entrance to Dutfield's Yard, the pony turned to the left and refused to go on. It was scared of something. Mr Diemschutz looked down to his right and in the pitch [2] darkness he could just see a shape on the ground. He got off his cart and struck a match. Before the breeze blew out the match he made out a figure in a dress: it was a woman.

Mr Diemschutz, anxious about the safety of his wife, went into the club to look for her. He found her safe with some club members and told them about the woman. Then he returned to the yard with a candle and a friend. When they saw a lot of blood flowing from the woman's neck, they ran to find a policeman. At the same time Morris Eagle, another member of the club, ran for help in the opposite direction. He found two policemen in Commercial Road, who rushed to Dutfield's Yard. Then one of them went off to bring a doctor. Edward Johnston, a doctor's assistant, arrived at 1.13. He examined the dead woman and saw that she had a deep cut in her throat. Her body was still warm. Dr Blackwell arrived at 1.16. He thought the woman had died between twenty to thirty minutes before. He noticed a scarf round her neck. It was tied on the left side and was pulled very tight. Had the killer seized [3] the scarf from behind and pulled her to the ground, where he cut her throat?

1. **accomplice** : person who helps another to do something illegal.
2. **pitch** : (here) complete.
3. **seized** : took hold of suddenly.

Detective Inspector Reid arrived at Dutfield's Yard at 1.45. He noted the dead woman's height – 1.57m – and guessed her age, about 42. She had curly dark-brown hair, a pale complexion, and light grey eyes. Two front teeth were missing at the top. She wore a long black jacket, and an old black skirt. Her stockings were white, her bonnet black, and she was wearing boots. There was one red rose on her jacket.

The witnesses identified the victim as the woman with the man near Dutfield's Yard. A man named Michael Kidney also identified her. He said she lived with him and her name was Elizabeth Stride. He had seen her for the last time on September 25th. Elizabeth sometimes stayed at a lodging house in Flower and Dean Street, where people called her Long Liz. Mrs Tanner, the deputy, said she last saw Elizabeth alive about 7 p.m. on Saturday 29th, in the kitchen of the lodging house.

Long Liz was born Elizabeth Gustafsdotter in 1843 near Gothenburg in Sweden. She probably came to England for domestic work. In 1869 she married John Stride, a carpenter. Nobody knows when the marriage broke down, but in 1877 Elizabeth was living in a workhouse. Her husband died in 1884, when Long Liz was lodging in Flower and Dean Street.

According to the medical evidence Elizabeth Stride died about 12.56 a.m., or even perhaps at 12.58. If this is true, Louis Diemschutz's arrival at 1 a.m. very probably disturbed the killer, so he only had time to cut his victim's throat. Then he hid in the darkness of Dutfield's Yard, and when Mr Diemschutz ran into the club, he quickly escaped. But the murder of Elizabeth Stride was not enough. Jack the Ripper wanted more blood, and he went to look for another victim.

Go back to the text

FCE **1 For questions 1-4, choose the answer (A, B, C or D) which you think fits best according to the text.**

1 At 12.30 some of the club members were
- A ☐ eating and drinking.
- B ☐ having a discussion.
- C ☐ singing.
- D ☐ going home.

2 There was some light
- A ☐ in the passage.
- B ☐ in the yard.
- C ☐ from the school.
- D ☐ from the street.

3 Constable Smith
- A ☐ walked along Berner Street every hour.
- B ☐ saw that the man had a newspaper.
- C ☐ noticed a man and a woman in Dutfield's Yard.
- D ☐ noticed that the woman had a red flower on her jacket.

4 Israel Schwartz crossed to the other side of the street
- A ☐ to help the woman.
- B ☐ because he wanted to avoid trouble.
- C ☐ before the first man shouted 'Lipski'.
- D ☐ because the man with the pipe followed him.

Reported speech: statements, questions, and orders

'I ***saw*** *a man stop and speak to a woman,' said Israel Schwartz.*
Israel Schwartz said ***he had seen*** *a man stop and speak to a woman.*
(reported statement)

*'****Are you*** *all right, dear?' Mr Diemschutz asked his wife.*
Mr Diemschutz asked his wife ***if she was*** *all right.*
(reported question)

*'****Go and bring*** *a doctor,' the policeman told his colleague.*
The policeman told his colleague ***to go and bring*** *a doctor.*
(reported order)

2 A Change the following into reported speech.

a. 'I saw a man and a woman by the school wall opposite the yard,' said Constable Smith.

b. 'Are you sure about the man's age?' the inspector asked Schwartz.

c. 'Did Mr Diemschutz disturb the killer?' the doctor wondered.

d. 'Bring me a candle, please,' Louis Diemschutz told his wife.

e. 'I saw Liz five days ago,' said Michael Kidney.

B Now change the following from reported speech to direct speech.

a. Morris Eagle told the policemen to follow him.

b. Inspector Abbeline thought the murderer had hidden in Dutfield's Yard.

c. Michael Kidney said her name was Elizabeth Stride, but people called her Long Liz because Long was a nickname for people with the surname Stride.

d. Inspector Reid asked the constable if he remembered when he had noticed the man and the woman.

e. Mrs Diemschutz told her husband not to go back into the yard.

3 Listening

Listen to the text and put the eight clocks in the correct order. Write 1, 2, 3, etc. in the boxes.

A

B

C

D

E

F

G

H

FCE **4** **For questions 1-4, complete the second sentence so that it has a similar meaning to the first sentence, using the word given. Do not change the word given. You must use between 2-5 words, including the word given. There is an example at the beginning (0).**

0 'I saw the man and the woman at 12.35,' said Constable Smith.
when
'It was 12.35 ....when I saw....... the man and the woman,' said Constable Smith.

1 There was a side door into the club kitchen in Dutfield's Yard.
that
The club had a side door .... the club kitchen.

2 The first man shouted 'Lipski', perhaps at Schwartz.
possible
It .... the first man shouted 'Lipski' at Schwartz.

3 The breeze blew out Mr Diemschutz's match.
by
Mr Diemschutz's match .... the breeze.

4 'I saw Liz at 7 o'clock last night,' said Mrs Tanner.
since
'I .... 7 o'clock last night,' said Mrs Tanner.

T: GRADE 7

5 **Topic — Village and city life**

London is a large city and at 1 o'clock in the morning lots of things are happening (even in 1888!). Do you think life in a village is very different? How? Find some information or pictures showing the main differences between village and city life. Keep these ideas in mind:

- Number and variety of people.
- Shopping and social facilities (cinema, sports centre, clubs, bars, etc.).
- Houses, flats, cottages, other types of buildings.
- Noise and pollution.

If you could choose, where would you live? Give reasons.

Cities mean loneliness, villages mean friends and neighbours. Discuss.

Before you read

FCE **1 For questions 1-12, read the text and decide which answer (A, B, C or D) best fits each space. There is an example at the beginning (0).**

(**0**) ...B..... the murder of Elizabeth Stride, Jack the Ripper went to look for (**1**) .... victim. He walked west towards the City of London. It is only twelve (**2**) .... walk from Berner Street to Mitre Square, where the second murder happened. (**3**) .... we do not know what time the killer arrived there, we know what his victim did and can (**4**) .... her movements on the night of September 29th/30th.

At 8.30 on Saturday night Constable Robinson (**5**) .... a woman lying on the pavement in Aldgate High Street. She was completely (**6**) .... (**7**) .... the help of another constable Robinson took her to Bishopsgate Street Police Station. She slept in a police cell (**8**) .... three hours. (**9**) .... she started singing quietly, and at 12.30 she asked the policeman on duty when she could (**10**) .... Twenty-five minutes later the policeman took her (**11**) .... her cell to the office. She asked him the time and he said nearly one o'clock, (**12**) .... was about the time of Elizabeth Stride's murder. The woman said her name was Mary Ann Kelly, but her real name was Catherine Eddowes.

0	**A** During	**B** After	**C** Before	**D** While
1	**A** the other	**B** other	**C** another	**D** others
2	**A** minute's	**B** minutes	**C** minute	**D** minutes'
3	**A** However	**B** Because	**C** Even	**D** Although
4	**A** to follow	**B** following	**C** follow	**D** follows
5	**A** find	**B** is finding	**C** found	**D** was finding
6	**A** drunk	**B** drink	**C** drank	**D** drinking
7	**A** By	**B** For	**C** With	**D** From
8	**A** since	**B** during	**C** before	**D** for
9	**A** As	**B** Then	**C** When	**D** So
10	**A** come	**B** stay	**C** go	**D** walk
11	**A** towards	**B** from	**C** at	**D** into
12	**A** that	**B** what	**C** when	**D** which

7 **Now listen to the beginning of Chapter Four and check your answers.**

CHAPTER **FOUR**

MITRE SQUARE

After the murder of Elizabeth Stride, Jack the Ripper went to look for another victim. He walked west towards the City of London. It is only twelve minutes' walk from Berner Street to Mitre Square, where the second murder happened. Although we do not know what time the killer arrived there, we know what his victim did and can follow her movements on the night of September 29/30th.

At 8.30 on Saturday night Constable Robinson found a woman lying on the pavement in Aldgate High Street. She was completely drunk. With the help of another constable Robinson took her to Bishopsgate Street Police Station. She slept in a police cell for three hours. Then she started singing quietly, and at 12.30 she asked the policeman on duty when she could go. Twenty-five minutes later the policeman took her from her cell to the office. She asked him the time and he said nearly one o'clock, which was about the time of Elizabeth Stride's murder.

The woman said her name was Mary Ann Kelly, but her real name was Catherine Eddowes.

'This way, miss,' said the policeman. He went with her to the street door and asked her to shut it when she left.

Catherine said, 'Good night.' And she went to meet her fate [1] at the hands of Jack the Ripper.

Mitre Square is eight minutes' walk from the police station. Perhaps Catherine arrived there at 1.10 a.m., perhaps later. We can imagine her singing to herself as she walked along, a small woman, about 1.52m, and thin. She looked about forty, and had dark brown hair under her black bonnet. Her clothes were old and dirty. She was wearing a red handkerchief around her neck, a black jacket, men's boots, and an old white apron. [2] This apron had an important part to play in the murder.

Around 1.33 three men came out of the Imperial Club in Duke Street. They passed a man and a woman at the corner of Church Passage that led into Mitre Square. The couple were talking quietly, and the woman had her hand on the man's chest. The place was badly-lit, but one man, Joseph Lawende, gave a description of them. He said the woman was short, and wore a black jacket and bonnet. The man was aged 30, 1.70m tall, medium build, with a fair complexion and moustache. He wore a grey cap with a peak, a red handkerchief around his neck, and had the appearance of a sailor. Mr Lawende told the police later, 'I don't think I can recognise him again.'

The three men passed on. The time was 1.35 a.m. Nine minutes later Constable Edward Watkins of the City Police

1. **fate** : something final or negative, such as death or defeat.
2. **apron** : piece of clothing worn on top of other clothes to keep them clean.

walked into Mitre Square. Everything seemed quiet. It was the same dark, silent square of 14 minutes before, when he had walked around it. But this time he got a terrible shock. In the darkest corner of the square he saw the body of a woman in the light of his lantern. He ran to a warehouse nearby and called out for the night watchman, a man named Morris. Mr Morris ran for assistance and soon returned with two policemen. Then Inspector Collard arrived from Bishopsgate Police Station, and Dr Brown came at 2.18 to examine the body.

There were also three plain-clothes detectives on the streets that night. They were part of the police hunt for the Whitechapel killer. At the time of the murder they were only a few streets away from Mitre Square. Hearing about the murder, they went to the square. Then they went off to look for the killer.

One of them walked through Goulston Street just before 2.15, but saw nothing suspicious and returned to Mitre Square. At 2.20 Constable Alfred Long also walked along Goulston Street and saw nothing unusual. His beat took him there approximately every thirty minutes, so at 2.55 he was back in Goulston Street. This time he saw a piece of bloodstained [1] apron in an open doorway. Near the piece of material, in white chalk on the wall, was a message:

The Juwes
are the Men
that will Not
be blamed
for nothing

1. **bloodstained** : discoloured with blood.

The Juwes
are the Men
That Will Not
be blamed
for nothi

When Constable Long reported this graffito, an Inspector McWilliam sent orders to photograph it. But the chief of the Metropolitan Police, Sir Charles Warren, changed the order. He was afraid about anti-Jewish demonstrations, so he ordered his men to rub out [1] the message. He destroyed an important clue. But he knew about the strong anti-semitic feelings in the area.

The piece of bloodstained apron fitted exactly into a missing section of the victim's apron. The killer evidently took it with him and cleaned his hands on it. At some time between 2.20 and 2.55 he was in Goulston Street. He threw the piece of apron, wet with blood, in the doorway and wrote the message. But perhaps he did not write the message. Perhaps it was already there and the murderer dropped the apron near it by chance. Or did he see the graffito and leave the apron there to put the blame on the Jews?

We shall never know the answer. But we know that Jack the Ripper was an extraordinary killer — cool, daring, and efficient. He came and went invisibly. Constable Watkins saw nothing in Mitre Square at 1.30. He did not see or hear anything when he entered it and discovered the body at 1.44. And only minutes before at 1.41 or 1.42 another officer looked into the square from Church Passage. 'I saw no one and heard no cry or noise,' he said later. Mr Morris, the night watchman in the warehouse, went to the door and looked into the square 'two moments' before Constable Watkins called him. Everything was quiet and deserted.

1. **rub out** : remove with water or a material.

MITRE SQUARE

So in less than fifteen minutes the Ripper took Catherine into Mitre square, killed her, mutilated her horribly, and escaped — right under the noses of the police! His escape was amazing. Immediately after the discovery of the murder the streets were full of policemen. The police were already everywhere in the area after Liz Stride's murder. But the discovery of the apron shows that the killer was out in the streets at some time between 2.20 and 2.55 — 36 to 71 minutes after Watkins discovered the body. Goulston Street is only five minutes from Mitre square. So what was the murderer doing? To the police Jack the Ripper was a mystery. He is still a mystery today.

Catherine Eddowes was the Ripper's fourth victim. She was 42 and lived in a lodging house. People said she was 'jolly', [1] always singing. Her partner was John Kelly. When they parted at 2 p.m. on Saturday 29th, Kelly told her to be careful about the Whitechapel killer.

'Don't you worry about me,' replied Catherine. 'I'll take care of myself, and I won't fall into his hands.'

1. **jolly** : full of fun.

Go back to the text

1 Summary

Put the sentences into the right order to make a summary of Chapter Four. Write 1, 2, 3, etc. in the correct boxes. Numbers 1 and 12 have been done for you.

a. [ ] Between 1.33 and 1.35 some men saw Catherine with a man near Mitre Square.

b. [ ] On the wall above the apron was a message which seemed to blame the Jews.

c. [ ] He went towards Mitre Square.

d. [ ] where she had been asleep in a cell for three hours.

e. [ ] Nine minutes later at 1.44 Constable Watkins found her body in the square.

f. [1] After killing Liz Stride, Jack the Ripper went to find another victim.

g. [ ] An hour later Constable Long found a piece of Catherine's bloodstained apron in Goulston Street.

h. [ ] Sir Charles Warren was worried about anti-Jewish demonstrations, so

i. [ ] At about the same time Catherine Eddowes left Bishopsgate Police Station,

j. [ ] The constable called out for a night watchman, who ran for assistance.

k. [12] The mysterious Ripper had claimed his fourth victim and escaped under the noses of the police!

l. [ ] he ordered his men to rub out the message.

FCE **2** **For questions 1-10, use the word given in capitals at the end of each line to form a word that fits in the space in the same line. There is an example at the beginning (0).**

Around 1.33 three men passed a man and a woman at	
the corner of Church Passage. The man and the woman	
were talking (**0**) ..quietly..... .	**QUIET**
The place was (**1**) .... -lit but one man, Joseph	**BAD**
Lawende, gave a (**2**) .... of them. He said the	**DESCRIBE**
man wore a peaked cap and had the (**3**) .... of a	**APPEAR**
sailor. Nine minutes later Constable Watkins found the	
body of a woman in the (**4**) .... corner of the	**DARK**
square. He called out for the night watchman of a	
warehouse, who ran for (**5**) .... Later, Inspector	**ASSIST**
Collard arrived, and Dr Brown made an (**6**)	**EXAM**
of the body.	
At 2.15 a plain-clothes (**7**) ...., who was walking	**DETECT**
through Goulston Street, saw nothing (**8**) .... At	**SUSPECT**
2.20 Constable Long also saw nothing (**9**) .... in	**USUAL**
the same street.	
But at 2.55 Constable Long saw a piece of (**10**)	**BLOOD**
apron in a doorway. Above it was a message written on	
the wall.	

3 **Vocabulary**

Complete the sentences with the adjectives in the box.

short badly-lit thin bloodstained daring jolly brown cool

a. Catherine Eddowes had dark .... hair, and was .... and ....

b. The entrance to Church Passage had one small lamp, so the place was ....

c. Jack the Ripper was a .... , ... killer because he took a lot of risks.

d. People said Catherine was .... because she sang and laughed.

e. The .... piece of apron exactly fitted the missing part of Catherine's apron.

4 Interview

You are interviewing Constable Watkins for a newspaper. Write questions using *what*, *where*, *when*, *how*, *why*, and *who*.

a. **You:** .... at 1.30?

Constable Watkins: I didn't see anything in the square at that time.

b. **You:** ....?

Constable Watkins: I discovered the body at 1.44.

c. **You:** ....?

Constable Watkins: In the darkest corner of the square.

d. **You:** ....?

Constable Watkins: By the light of my lantern.

e. **You:** ....?

Constable Watkins: I felt very shocked, of course.

f. **You:** ....?

Constable Watkins: I ran to a warehouse and called out for the night watchman.

g. **You:** ....?

Constable Watkins: I don't know, but it was an amazing escape because policemen were everywhere.

h. **You:** ....?

Constable Watkins: We don't know. Perhaps the murderer wrote it, perhaps not.

i. **You:** ....?

Constable Watkins: Who knows? Perhaps he killed her because he hates women.

j. **You:** ....?

Constable Watkins: Jack the Ripper, of course, the same man who killed the other women.

FCE 5 Writing

You have seen this notice in the *Star* newspaper.

Did you know Catherine Eddowes?

We need reliable information about the Whitechapel killer's latest victim.

If you know anything about her past life, we would like to hear from you.

Please write and send your information to us.

Your name will be kept strictly confidential.

Imagine you are Catherine Eddowes's daughter Annie. Write a reply to the notice above of 120-180 words using the information given below.

- Born 14th April 1842, Wolverhampton.
- Parents George and Catharine. Religion Catholic. Eleven children.
- Family moved to London December 1844.
- Educated at St John's Charity School, London.
- 1855 Mother died. Family broke up. Kate (Catherine) sent to live with aunt in Wolverhampton. Kate not happy with aunt, ran away to Birmingham.
- 1858 Living with a man named Thomas Conway.
- 1865 Daughter Annie born.
- 1868-73 Two sons born.
- 1880 Moved back to London. Kate drinking a lot. Separated from Conway.
- 1881 Met John Kelly in lodgings in Flower and Dean Street. Started living together there.
- 1886 Daughter Annie moved to another house but did not give Catherine her new address.
- 1888 Annie has not seen her mother for two years.

Immigrants *in the East End*

The East End has a long history of immigration. French Huguenots[1] and Jews from Spain came in the 17th century, Irish escaped the

Irish emigrants waiting for a train (1864) by Erskine Nicol.

1. **Huguenots** : French Protestants of the 16-17th century, many of whom suffered severe persecution for their faith.

potato famine in the 1850s and worked as labourers in the London Docks, and German immigrants worked in the production of sugar. Then, in the 1880s, began the largest immigration of Jews from Eastern Europe. They introduced their own language and customs, dress, food, clubs and synagogues. The witness Joseph Lawende belonged to the Imperial Club, which was Jewish. Israel Schwartz was Hungarian, Louis Diemschutz was Russian, and his friend Isaac Kozebrodsky was Polish; they were all Jews. They lived in cheap lodgings and worked in the markets, shops and factories. There were mainly Irish and Jews trading in Whitechapel market, one of the largest in England. When the trade in second-hand clothes moved to Whitechapel, Petticoat Lane market in Middlesex Street became a Jewish market for clothes. These people became important for the economy of the East End.

AT THE DOCKS: ARRIVALS BY A GERMAN STEAMER.

Arrivals by German boat (1900).

Jews in front of a barber's shop in London (20th century).

The arrival of so many foreigners caused a lot of tension in the area, and this played an important part in the Whitechapel murders. It seemed that the killer tried to incriminate the Jews. Was he really anti-Jewish or did he try to deceive the police by blaming the Jews? The police foolishly destroyed a vital clue (the message in Goulston Street) because they did not want any anti-Jewish trouble.

However, they arrested several foreigners as suspects. A German, Charles Ludwig, was arrested after threatening a woman with a knife on September 18th. Another suspect was Joseph Isenschmid, a lunatic who carried large knives with him in the streets late at night and disappeared after Annie Chapman's murder. He was arrested on September 12th. But he was not the Ripper; he was in police custody during the later murders.

Some police officers suspected a Pole called Aaron Kosminski. But he was a mad tramp who never washed, heard voices in his head, and ate bread from the streets. This man does not fit the type of ruthless killer that the Ripper was. Kosminski died in a lunatic asylum in 1919.

Immigration to London's East End still continues today, particularly around Brick Lane. The latest immigrants are Bangladeshis.

A market in the East End of London.

1 Answer these questions.

a. Why did many Irish emigrate to England in the 1850s?
b. Where did the immigrants in the 1880s come from? Name some countries.
c. What kind of market was Petticoat Lane?
d. How did immigration play a part in the Whitechapel murders?
e. Why did the police arrest Charles Ludwig?
f. Why was Jacob Isenschmid suspected?
g. Where was Isenschmid at the time of the double murder (September 30th)?
h. What type of person was Aaron Kosminski?

Before you read

1 Listening

FCE

Listen to the beginning of Chapter Five and complete the sentences.

1 Mary Jane Kelly's .... when she was very young.

2 When Mary was sixteen, she married a miner who .... in the mines.

3 We do not know why ....

4 After Mary met Joe Barnett, they ....

5 .... they were renting a room in Miller's Court.

6 Mary .... if she drank too much.

7 On October 30th 1888 Joe ....

8 Joe was unemployed, so .... the rent.

9 On the evening of 8th November Joe visited Mary to tell her ....

10 Maria Harvey .... in Mary's room at Miller's Court.

11 When Maria went soon after Joe's arrival, she left ....

Now read the text and check your answers.

CHAPTER **FIVE**

THE WORK OF A DEVIL

1 Mary Jane Kelly was twenty-five years old. Born in Limerick, Ireland, she moved to Wales with her family when she was very young. At sixteen she married a miner named Davies, who was killed in an explosion in the mines. Mary came to London in 1884. By 1886 she was living in the East End with Joe Flemming, who wanted to marry her. Nobody knows why she did not marry him. However, in 1887 she met Joe Barnett, a porter at Billingsgate fish market. At the time she was living at Cooley's lodging house in Thrawl Street. Mary and Barnett decided to live together, and by the beginning of 1888 they were renting a room, 13 Miller's Court in Dorset Street.

2 Descriptions of Mary suggest an attractive young woman, about 1.70m tall, with a stout [1] build, blue eyes, and a complexion 'as fair as a lily'. She was pleasant when sober but she could be noisy and very quarrelsome [2] when drunk. In fact, Joe Barnett walked out after a quarrel on October 30th. He was a reliable, kind man who did not want Mary to go out on the streets. Unfortunately he had not worked for some months so the couple

1. **stout** : strong and solidly built.
2. **quarrelsome** : inclined to quarrel or disagree.

could not pay the rent, and Mary had returned to prostitution. This was one of the reasons why they quarrelled that autumn.

Nevertheless, Mary and Barnett remained friends. He frequently visited her and gave her money. He visited her around 7.30-7.45 on the evening of Thursday, November 8th to tell her he had no work and could not give her any money. Mary's friend, a laundress [1] named Maria Harvey, was there and said that Mary and Barnett seemed to be friendly. She went soon after Barnett's arrival, leaving some clothing, which included a man's overcoat, some shirts, a petticoat, and a bonnet. END

3 When Barnett left at about 8 p.m., Mary knew she had to go out into the streets to earn some money. Nearly four hours later Mary Ann Cox, who lived in Miller's Court, saw Mary walking along Dorset Street with a man. Mrs Cox followed them into the court and said, 'Goodnight, Mary Jane' as they were going into Mary's room. Mary was so drunk that she could not answer properly. Mrs Cox saw the stranger in the light of the gas lamp opposite Mary's front door. He was about thirty-six, 1.65m tall, stout, with a carrot-coloured moustache. He had a bottle of beer in his hand. As she went indoors [2] Mrs Cox heard Mary singing an Irish song.

Just after midnight Mrs Cox went out. When she came back at 1 a.m., there was a light in number 13 and Mary was still singing. After warming her hands, Mrs Cox went out again. Returning at 3 o'clock, she saw no light in Mary's room, and all was quiet. That night it rained hard and Mrs Cox could not sleep well. Although men went in and out of the court, she did not hear anything suspicious. But another witness told a different story.

1. **laundress** : woman who washes other people's clothes for money.
2. **indoors** : inside a house or building.

THE WORK OF A DEVIL

4 Elizabeth Prater lived above Mary's room. She went to bed about 1.30 a.m. and fell asleep. Around two hours later she woke up suddenly because her kitten was walking over her. She guessed the time was about 3.30-4.00. At that moment she heard 'screams of "Murder!" two or three times in a female voice'. She later changed this to a quiet cry of 'Oh! Murder!' Mrs Prater said she went back to sleep; she often heard cries of murder in the court.

When Sarah Lewis passed Christ Church near Dorset Street, the church clock struck 2.30. Mrs Lewis was going to stay with her friends at 2 Miller's Court. She slept badly in a chair until 3.30, when she heard the clock strike, and was awake until nearly five o'clock. Just before 4 a.m. a young woman screamed 'Murder!' not far away. Mrs Lewis did nothing because cries like this were usual in Whitechapel. It is probable that Mrs Prater and Mrs Lewis paid no attention to Mary Kelly's last terrified cry for help!

5 Friday November 9th was the day when the citizens of London celebrated the Lord Mayor's Show. 'I hope it will be a fine day tomorrow,' Mary had told Mrs Prater the morning before, 'as I want to go to the Lord Mayor's Show.' At 10.45 on Friday morning Mary's landlord, John McCarthy, was checking his accounts in his shop at 27 Dorset Street. He noticed that Mary owed him 29 shillings [1] in rent, so he sent his assistant Thomas Bowyer to her room to ask for the money. Bowyer got no answer when he knocked twice. He walked to his right round the corner, where there were two windows of number 13. The window nearest to the door was broken in two places. Bowyer put his hand in and pulled back the curtain. The first thing he saw was two pieces of

1. **shillings** : units of money used in Britain until 1971. 1 shilling = 5 pence.

flesh on the bedside table. Then he saw a body lying on the bed and a lot of blood. He ran back to the shop to tell McCarthy.

6 When McCarthy looked through the window, his face turned pale. The body on the bed resembled something in a butcher's shop. He told Bowyer to go to Commercial Street Police Station. Inspectors Beck and Dew, the detectives on duty, went to the murder scene. The door was locked. Inspector Abbeline arrived at 11.30 a.m., but he could not give the order to break open the door until 1.30 p.m. He had to wait for some bloodhound dogs to arrive. At 1.30 when the news came that the dogs were not coming, he told McCarthy to break open the door. Nobody knew that it was not necessary. Barnett and Mary used to put a hand through the broken window and pull back the bolt[1] to open the door.

7 The scene in the little room was from a nightmare. It was only 4-5 metres square and the door banged against the bedside table. There was not much furniture: an old table and two old chairs stood on the bare, dirty floor. In the fireplace were the ashes of a large fire. On the bed lay a body that was almost unrecognisable. Only the hair and eyes identified it as Mary Kelly. John McCarthy said later, 'It looked more like the work of a devil than of a man.' And Mrs Prater, who looked through the window, said, 'I can never forget it if I live to be a hundred.'

8 Next day Inspector Abbeline examined the ashes in the fireplace. The strong heat from the fire had melted part of a kettle.[2] In the ashes Abbeline found some women's clothing, which Maria Harvey had left in the room. Why had the Ripper burnt them? When Abbeline discovered only one small piece of

1. **bolt** : metal bar that slides across to lock a door or window.
2. **kettle** : container used to boil water.

candle in the room, he thought that the killer had made a fire with the clothes because he needed more light to do his terrible work.

This time Jack the Ripper had time to finish his crime without interruption. It was truly the work of a devil.

Go back to the text

1 Summary

Chapter Five has been divided into 8 parts. Choose from the list A-I the sentence which best summarises each part (1-8). There is one extra sentence which you do not need to use.

A ☐ Hear screams, do nothing!
B ☐ An hour of song, then silence
C ☐ View through a window — for 29 shillings
D ☐ The short road to Miller's Court
E ☐ Murder by the light of fire
F ☐ The butcher's shop is closed
G ☐ Quarrelsome Mary and unemployed Joe
H ☐ They paid no attention to 'Murder!'
I ☐ Inside number 13 Miller's Court

2 Prepositions

Complete the following sentences using the prepositions in the box.

against	**through(x2)**	**up**	**out(x2)**
for	**back(x5)**	**down**	**over**

a. Thomas Bowyer pulled .... the curtain and looked .... the window.

b. The kitten walked .... Mrs Prater and woke her ....

c. John McCarthy finally broke .... the door at 1.30.

d. Mrs Prater went .... to sleep because she often heard cries of murder.

e. The landlord sent his assistant to ask .... the rent.

f. 'If you put your hand .... the window, you can pull .... the bolt,' Barnett told Abbeline.

g. After quarrelling with Mary on October 30th, Joe walked ....

h. The door of number 13 knocked .... the bedside table.

i. Mrs Cox went .... after midnight and came .... at 1am.

j. When Thomas Bowyer saw all the blood, he ran .... to the shop.

9 3 Listening

Would you like to go on a Ripper Walk? Listen to the text and draw the route on the map. As you follow, number the boxes on the route 1, 2, 3, etc. to show who was murdered there.

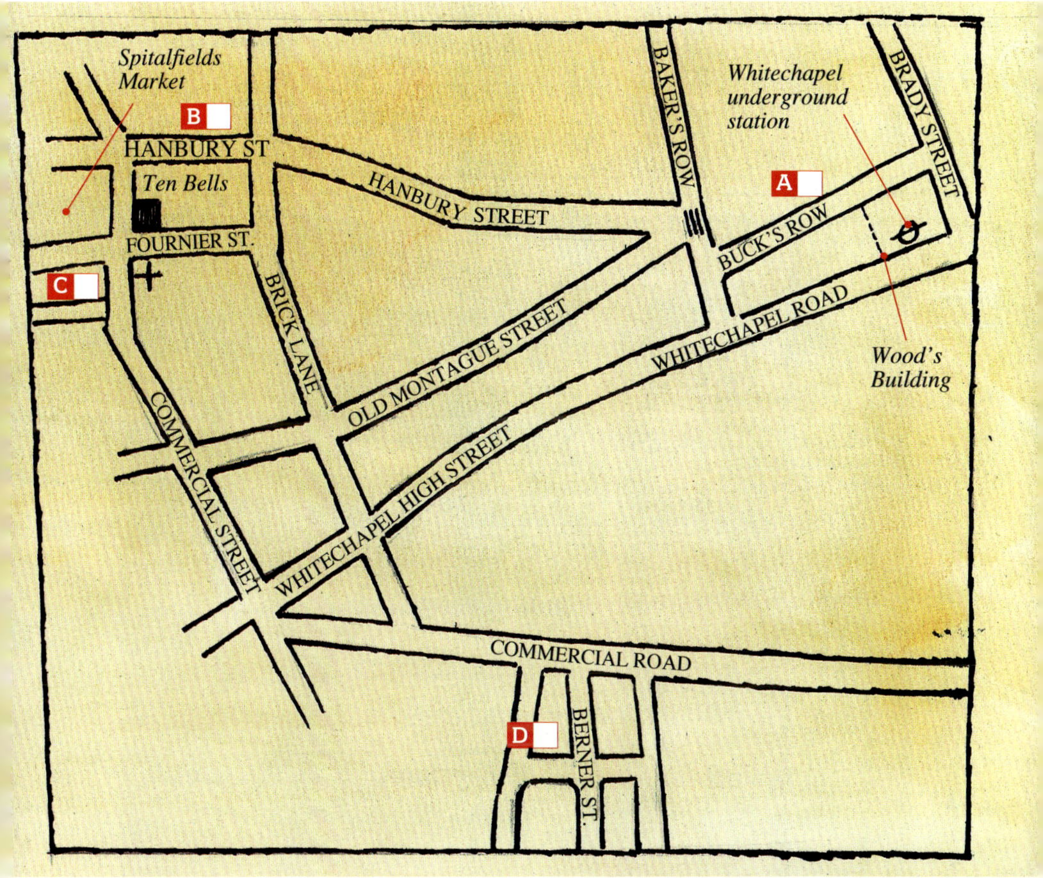

1. Annie Chapman
2. Elizabeth Stride
3. Mary Kelly
4. Polly Nichols

INTERNET PROJECT

Let's find some more information about a Ripper Walk and the Ripper case.
Connect to the Internet and go to www.blackcat-cideb.com or www.cideb.it.
Insert the title or part of the title of the book into our search engine.
Open the page for *Jack the Ripper*. Click on the internet project link. Go down the page until you find the title of this book and click on the relevant link for this project.
Organise your class into two groups. Each group can report to the class on one of the following:

- An organised Ripper Walk
- Documents and other details about the case

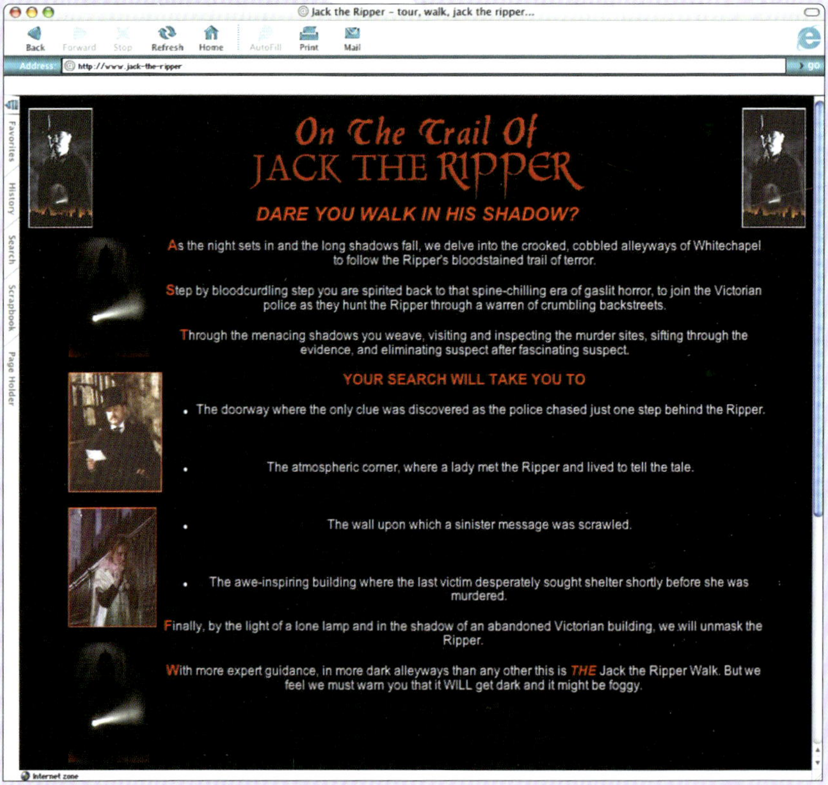

T: GRADE 7

4 Topic – National and local customs

The Lord Mayor's Show is an old English custom from medieval times. Is there a Lord Mayor's Show where you live? If not, find some information or pictures showing some national customs in your country. Tell the class about them using these questions to help you.

a. How old is the custom and what are its origins?

b. How is the custom celebrated? Describe any rituals or ceremonies.

c. What do you like most about the customs?

d. Do you think national customs are necessary or useful? Why/Why not?

Before you read

FCE **1 Read the text and think of the word which best fits each space. Use only one word in each space. There is an example at the beginning (0).**

The man called Jack the Ripper (**0**) ......was...... never caught, and his name will probably (**1**) .... be known. There were (**2**) .... of suspects at the time, but the police did not have (**3**) .... real evidence against (**4**) .... During the years since the (**5**) .... the number of suspects has increased.
An identikit picture of the Ripper can (**6**) .... constructed from the descriptions by the few witnesses who possibly (**7**) .... him. The first witness was Elizabeth Darrell, (**8**) .... very probably saw the Ripper with Annie Chapman outside 29 Hanbury Street. He wore a brown deerstalker (**9**) .... and was short, about 1.63m. Mrs Darrell (**10**) .... not see his face, so her impression that he was a dark-looking foreigner aged over forty is (**11**) .... certain.

10 **Now listen to the beginning of Chapter Six and check your answers.**

CHAPTER **SIX**

WHO WAS JACK THE RIPPER?

10 The man called Jack the Ripper was never caught, and his name will probably never be known. There were lots of suspects at the time, but the police did not have any real evidence against them. During the years since the murders the number of suspects has increased.

An identikit picture of the man can be constructed from the descriptions by the few witnesses who possibly saw him. The first witness was Elizabeth Darrell, who very probably saw the Ripper with Annie Chapman outside 29 Hanbury Street. He wore a brown deerstalker hat and was short, about 1.63m. Mrs Darrell did not see his face, so her impression that he was a dark-looking foreigner aged over forty is not certain. END

In the case of Elizabeth Stride, from the descriptions by Constable Smith and Israel Schwartz we have a man between 28-30 years old, 1.65m to 1.70m tall, wearing dark clothes and a hat with a peak, or perhaps a deerstalker. Schwartz said the man

Maud Marsh. He had killed other women in the same way. Chapman's real name was Severiano Klosowski, a Polish immigrant working as a barber in Whitechapel in 1888. But he had only arrived in England the year before, so how could he know the area as well as the Ripper? And is it possible that Jack the Ripper changed from savagely killing prostitutes to poisoning barmaids?

A recent suspect is the famous artist Walter Sickert, known as the British Impressionist. He was 28 years old and living in London at the time of the murders. His strange character has attracted suspicion. He was secretive and often disappeared into dark little rented rooms around the poor quarters of London. He had a morbid interest in the Ripper murders all his life, and it is possible that he sent 'Ripper' letters to the police. But there is no real evidence to connect him with the killings. He was also taller and slimmer than the man described by witnesses. His gloomy paintings of murder scenes were part of his vision as an artist: he liked to paint the dark, squalid side of life. Other artists and writers show a similar fascination with violence – Dickens, for example, or Zola. But that does not mean they are murderers.

A more probable suspect is George Hutchinson (mentioned earlier). He gave a detailed statement on the evening of November 12th, after the inquest on Mary Kelly. Some writers have asked why he did not go to the police before the inquest. Was it because Mrs Lewis's testimony appeared in the newspapers only after the inquest? When he read the report, he realised that she had seen him opposite Miller's Court. So he had to go to the police before they found him and asked him why he was there. Did he make a false statement and give a false description? Did he have something to hide?

FCE 2 Characters

What do you remember about the people in Chapter Six? Of which of the people (A-F) are the following true? There is an example at the beginning (0).

A	Jack the Ripper	**B**	Elizabeth Darrell
C	George Hutchinson	**D**	Montague John Druitt
E	George Chapman	**F**	Inspector Abbeline

Who ...

0 [B] saw the Ripper in Hanbury Street?
1 [ ] liked playing sports?
2 [ ] believed Hutchinson's story?
3 [ ] thought the Ripper was perhaps foreign?
4 [ ] poisoned a woman who worked in his pub?
5 [ ] was seen standing opposite Miller's Court?
6 [ ] lost his job in a school?
7 [ ] liked wearing a peaked hat?
8 [ ] followed Mary Kelly and her client?
9 [ ] suspected George Chapman of being the Ripper?
10 [ ] came to England in 1887?
11 [ ] had very little medical skill?
12 [ ] threw himself into the Thames?

3 Suspects

Complete the text with the words provided.

moustache dark peak muscles deerstalker doctor
stout picture butcher witnesses suspect professional

Jack the Ripper was never caught, but an identikit [1]...................... can be built from the descriptions by the [2]...................... who possibly saw him. He was probably a short, [3]...................... man with strong [4]...................... . He had a small, light brown [5]...................... .

He liked wearing [6]...................... clothes and often wore a cap with one [7]...................... , like a sailor's, or with two, like a [8]...................... .

He probably worked as a labourer, a [9]...................... , or perhaps a clerk. He was certainly not from the royal family, the aristocracy, or the [10]...................... class, like a [11]...................... . So Montague Druitt and Walter Sickert do not qualify as the killer. According to a recent theory, the most probable [12]...................... is a labourer called George Hutchinson.

11

4 Listening – Identify the suspect

Now look at the identikit pictures. Which man fits the description? Tick (✓) the appropriate box.

A ☐

B ☐

C ☐

D ☐

5 Writing

Using the ideas below, write about Jack the Ripper in about 120-180 words.

a. Solitary/no accomplice?
b. Killed at weekends/employed/butcher?
c. Doctor/surgeon?
d. Married?
e. Lived or worked where?
f. Knew two of his victims?

Before you read

12 FCE

1 Listening

Listen to the beginning of Chapter Seven and decide whether the statements are true (T) or false (F).

		T	F
1	The Whitechapel murders were more shocking in 1888 than they are today.	☐	☐
2	Murders like those of the Ripper had been known before.	☐	☐
3	The general opinion was that the killer was a lunatic.	☐	☐
4	Martha Tabram's murder was certainly the Ripper's work.	☐	☐
5	People paid no attention to the sensational reports in the newspapers.	☐	☐
6	The Ripper murders both scared and fascinated people.	☐	☐
7	'Leather Apron' was an alias for Jack the Ripper.	☐	☐
8	John Pizer was hunted by the police for demanding money from women.	☐	☐
9	Pizer was arrested because he wore a leather apron.	☐	☐
10	Pizer proved that he had not murdered Annie Chapman.	☐	☐

Now read the text and check your answers.

CHAPTER **SEVEN**

PANIC!

12 In our violent times it is difficult to imagine the shock and horror that the Whitechapel murders caused in 1888. In Victorian times the East End was also violent, but the Ripper murders were something new. Murder was usually the result of domestic quarrels, drink, or robbery. The Ripper murders were the first of a new kind of crime: serial killings, savage, without an obvious motive, no clues, and very difficult to solve.

The fury of the Ripper's way of killing puzzled the doctors, the police, the public and the press. To them he was a lunatic. On August 7th, before the Buck's Row murder, a woman called Martha Tabram was killed and then stabbed ferociously with a knife 39 times. This was so unusual that some writers today believe it was a Ripper murder. At the time the newspapers called it 'unique and mysterious' and the work of a homicidal maniac.

After the Polly Nichols murder, sensational reports in the newspapers increased the public's fear and horror. Women became very nervous. People discussed it in the streets and large crowds visited Buck's Row on September 4th. There were stories of a mysterious man known as 'Leather Apron', who demanded money from prostitutes and beat them if they resisted. When the police found a leather apron at the scene of the Hanbury Street murder, they hunted a man called John Pizer, a Polish boot-maker who always wore a leather apron for his work. They found him hiding with his family and arrested him on September 10th. But he had a very good alibi, which proved his innocence.

After the Hanbury Street murder people waited in queues outside newsagents. The *Star* reported the crime in very sensational language: the killer was 'half beast, half man', a 'demon', or 'vampire'. When Mrs Mary Burridge of south London read about the murder, she collapsed and died of fright. The East End community fell into panic and hysteria. On September 8th thousands of frightened people were out in the streets. Large angry crowds gathered in Hanbury Street and at the local police stations. They attacked anybody who looked suspicious. A young criminal called Squibby, for example, was in Hanbury Street, when a detective saw him in the crowd and chased him. The crowd followed shouting, 'Catch him!' Squibby was terrified and finally surrendered to the police for his own protection.

The anger of the crowd also turned against Jews, who were threatened and abused. Liz Stride and Kate Eddowes were murdered near Jewish clubs, and the police were very nervous about the possibility of anti-Jewish disturbances. The message in chalk that blamed the Jews was written on the wall of a building in a Jewish area. But it is certain that the Ripper was not Jewish,

and Samuel Montague, an important Jewish citizen and MP, [1] offered a reward of £100 for the arrest of the murderer. Also, some Jewish tradesmen organised a vigilance committee to help the police and offered a reward.

At night, anger changed to terror. Shops closed early; people rushed home and locked their doors. Some prostitutes left Whitechapel. Panic spread all over London. When a man called Brennan began to shout about the murders in a pub in Camberwell, the customers ran out into the street and Brennan was soon arrested. But in Whitechapel the pubs were empty, and there were only policemen and vagabonds in the dark streets. Calm began to return only after a few weeks.

Meanwhile, the newspapers continued to report sensational stories and rumours. But they could not print details of the killer's mutilations, which the doctor did not reveal. Although the details of Annie Chapman's murder were given on September 19th, they were not reported for reasons of decency. However, two days before, somebody sent a letter to the police, which was never published. It began 'Dear Boss' and there was a postscript which included the sentence 'What a pretty necklace I gave her'. The writer was probably talking about the injury to Annie's throat, but only the police, the doctors and the killer knew the details of Annie's murder. The letter was signed 'Catch me if you can. Jack the Ripper'. It was very probably from the murderer. A second letter of September 27th was signed 'Yours truly, Jack the Ripper'. This was published on October 1st, the day that the world finally had a name for the Whitechapel killer.

1. **MP** : Member of Parliament.

PANIC!

After the double murder of September 30th the panic got worse. By 11 o'clock that morning, one reporter wrote, it seemed that the whole of the East End was 'out of doors'. Thousands of people went to Berner Street and Mitre Square. Many of them paid to look at the murder scenes from windows. Sellers of fruit, sweets and nuts did a fabulous trade. But on October 3rd shopkeepers complained that they were losing a lot of business because people were afraid to go out shopping.

During the following weeks sales of newspapers, and verses and songs about the murders were enormous. Women lived in terror. Some hoaxers [1] pretended to be the Ripper and followed women to scare them. On October 10th a woman hanged herself at 65 Hanbury Street because she was depressed about the murders. Thousands of letters offering information and help were sent to Scotland Yard. Inspector Abbeline and his colleagues had to read all of them. Abbeline himself walked around the Whitechapel Streets until four or five in the morning. He worked very hard and nearly had a nervous breakdown.

Hundreds of extra police patrolled the area, some dressed as women. Lodgers, butchers, and slaughterers [2] were questioned. On October 13th the police began to search every house in a certain radius of the crimes. The search ended on the 18th, and the police admitted they had not found the smallest clue. But it is very possible that they interviewed Jack the Ripper.

Years later Detective Walter Dew wrote in his memoirs about the killer's 'amazing elusiveness'. Jack the Ripper is still as elusive today as he was in 1888.

1. **hoaxers** : people who carry out humorous or malicious tricks.
2. **slaughterers** [slɔːtərɜːz] : men whose job is to kill animals for food (in a slaughterhouse).

Go back to the text

FCE **1** **For questions 1-5, choose the answer (A, B, C or D) which you think fits best according to the text.**

1 The newspaper reports

- A ☐ were moderate and responsible.
- B ☐ encouraged feelings of panic.
- C ☐ were anxious about women.
- D ☐ described details of the mutilations.

2 After the Hanbury Street murder

- A ☐ angry crowds killed Mrs Burridge.
- B ☐ the newspapers attacked innocent people.
- C ☐ panic spread through the East End.
- D ☐ a criminal called Squibby was killed by the crowd.

3 During the panic the only people in the streets at night were

- A ☐ shoppers.
- B ☐ pub customers.
- C ☐ women.
- D ☐ policemen and vagabonds.

4 On September 17th who knew about the details of Annie's murder?

- A ☐ the Press
- B ☐ only the doctors
- C ☐ the police, the doctors, and the murderer
- D ☐ the murderer and the police

5 In October the police

- A ☐ worked hard to find the killer.
- B ☐ followed women.
- C ☐ interviewed Jack the Ripper.
- D ☐ found some small clues.

2 **Can you complete these sentences with information from Chapter Seven?**

a. In Victorian times murders were usually caused by ....

b. Some modern writers believe Martha Tabram was a Ripper victim because ....

c. The police hunted John Pizer because ....

d. Squibby was terrified and asked the police ....

e. When people began to blame Jews for the crimes, Samuel Montague ....

f. The world finally got a name for the killer when ....

g. Abbeline worked so hard on the Ripper case ....

FCE **3** **Read the text from Chapter 7 below and think of the word which best fits the gap. Use only one word in each gap. There is an example at the beginning (0).**

During the following weeks sales of the newspapers, and verses and songs (**0**) ...about.... the murders were enormous. Women lived in terror. Some hoaxers pretended to be the Ripper and followed women to scare (**1**) ....

On October 10th a woman hanged (**2**) .... at 65 Hanbury Street because she was depressed about the murders. Thousands of letters offering information and help (**3**) .... sent to Scotland yard. Inspector Abbeline and his colleagues (**4**) .... to read all of them. Abbeline himself walked (**5**) .... the Whitechapel streets until four or five in the morning. He worked very (**6**) .... and nearly had a nervous breakdown.

Hundreds of extra police patrolled the area, some dressed (**7**) .... women. Lodgers, butchers, and slaughterers were questioned. After a search (**8**) .... the area, the police admitted they had not found (**9**) .... clues. But it is very possible (**10**) .... they interviewed Jack the Ripper.

Years later Detective Walter Dew wrote (**11**) .... his memoirs about the killer's 'amazing elusiveness'. Jack the Ripper is (**12**) .... as elusive today as he was in 1888.

13 4 Listen and match

Listen to the text and match the events to the dates. Write a, b, c, etc. in the box next to the correct date. The first one has been done for you.

1. [g] August 7th
2. [ ] August 31st
3. [ ] September 8th
4. [ ] September 17th
5. [ ] September 27th
6. [ ] September 30th
7. [ ] October 1st
8. [ ] October 10th
9. [ ] October 13th-18th

a. Second letter sent.
b. Hanbury Street murder.
c. Woman hanged herself.
d. First letter sent.
e. Double murder.
f. Second letter published.
g. ~~Martha Tabram murdered.~~
h. Police search houses.
i. Murder of Polly Nichols.

FCE 5 Writing

Imagine you are Inspector Abbeline in retirement. You are writing a book about your career (your memoirs), which includes the events of October 1888. Using information from the text, write 120-180 words in an appropriate style.
Include the following:

- Scenes in Berner Street and Mitre Square
- Hoaxers following women
- Reading a huge number of letters/filing information
- Walking the streets of Whitechapel in the early hours
- Policemen patrolling the streets dressed as women
- Questioning people, searching houses, etc.

FCE 1 **Summary**

A For questions 1-25, read this summary of the Ripper murders and think of the word which best fits each space. There is an example at the beginning (0).

In the East End of London **(0)** .....in........... the autumn of 1888 a man known **(1)** .... Jack the Ripper murdered at least five women. The first victim was Polly Nichols. Her body **(2)** .... found in Buck's Row in the **(3)** .... morning of August 31st. The killer murdered his first victim quickly and silently. He left **(4)** .... clues and **(5)** .... was no motive. The police could not **(6)** .... this new kind of murder.

The killer killed **(7)** .... on September 8th in the back **(8)** .... of 29 Hanbury Street. John Davis discovered the mutilated body of Annie Chapman at 6 a.m. This time the killer **(9)** .... attacked in daylight. **(10)** .... one witness, Mrs Darrell, probably saw him just **(11)** .... the murder, she did not see **(12)** .... face.

On September 30th the Whitechapel murderer killed twice. Elizabeth Stride was the first **(13)** .... She was murdered in Berner Street between 12.50-12.58. Her body was discovered **(14)** .... Louis Diemschutz at 1 a.m., **(15)** .... perhaps he interrupted the killer. A witness named Israel Schwartz possibly **(16)** .... the murderer at 12.45.

Then the Ripper went to look **(17)** .... another victim. He killed Catherine Eddowes in Mitre Square at **(18)** .... 1.40. **(19)** .... mutilated body was found at 1.44. At 2.55 Constable Long found a **(20)** .... of Catherine's apron in Goulston Street, not **(21)** .... from Mitre Square. There was a message **(22)** .... in chalk above the apron which seemed to blame the Jews for the murders. The Police Commissioner ordered the message to **(23)** .... rubbed out **(24)** .... he was worried about anti-Jewish demonstrations. Jack the Ripper had murdered two women in one night and escaped right under the **(25)** .... of the police!

B Now finish the summary in your own words. Use these ideas as a guide.

- Mrs Cox's testimony
- Elizabeth Prater's testimony
- Sarah Lewis's testimony
- George Hutchinson
- John McCarthy and Thomas Bowyer's discovery
- Inspector Abbeline's theory about the fire

2 Answer the following questions.

a. How much real evidence is there against many of the suspects?
b. Give one reason why George Hutchinson is a possible suspect.
c. How did the newspapers help to create panic?
d. What was the atmosphere like in London after the double murder?
e. What kinds of people did the police interview in October?
f. Why couldn't the press print details of the killer's mutilations of his victims?
g. Who gave the killer the name 'Jack the Ripper'?
h. Why did Abbeline nearly have a nervous breakdown?
i. 'What a pretty necklace I gave her.' What was the killer talking about?
j. Why did Inspector Dew write about the murderer's 'elusiveness'?

KEY TO EXIT TEST

1A 1. as **2.** was **3.** early **4.** no **5.** there **6.** understand **7.** again **8.** yard **9.** had **10.** although **11.** before **12.** his **13.** victim **14.** by **15.** so **16.** saw **17.** for **18.** about **19.** Her **20.** piece **21.** far **22.** written **23.** be **24.** because/as **25.** noses

2 a. Not much/None. **b.** His age and appearance are similar to descriptions of the Ripper. **c.** They wrote sensational reports and rumours. **d.** Panic, women in terror, only police in the streets, shops closed. **e.** Lodgers, butchers, and slaughterers. **f.** The doctors did not give the details for reasons of decency. **g.** The murderer himself. **h.** He overworked/worked very hard. **i.** Probably the injury to his victim's throat. **j.** Because the killer left no clues and was never caught.